The Quiet Place

A One-Act Play

By

EDDIE KENNEDY

THE DRAMATIC PUBLISHING COMPANY

Printed in the United States of America

(THE QUIET PLACE)

ISBN 0-87129-456-7

THE QUIET PLACE

A One-Act Play
for Three Men, Four Women

CHARACTERS

SHEILA . . . . a teenage girl

PAM, JANET . . . . Sheila's friends

DAVID . . . . older brother of Sheila's boyfriend

PATSY, TONY, STEVE . . . . high school gang members

TIME: The Present
PLACE: A small hillside in early spring

THE QUIET PLACE

AT RISE OF CURTAIN: The lights come up on a small hillside which has a stone bench off to one side, and a tree stump to the other. It is early spring, but there is still a chill in the air. The sound of the wind and birds quietly sweeps the hill. SHEILA, a teenage girl, sits alone on the bench. She sits quietly, obviously distressed. After a moment, she wipes her eyes and places the handkerchief in her jacket pocket. PAM and JANET enter quickly and stop when they see SHEILA. They appear nervous. After a slight hesitation, JANET moves toward SHEILA while PAM holds back, as if keeping watch.

JANET. Sheila?
SHEILA (turning). Yes?
JANET. We thought you might be here.
SHEILA. Yeah.
PAM. Are you all right?
SHEILA. I'm fine, Pam.
PAM. Are you sure?
SHEILA (rising). I'm sure.
JANET (after a pause). It's kinda cold, isn't it?
SHEILA. Yes, it is.

JANET. Are you warm enough?

SHEILA. I'm fine, Janet, thank you.

JANET. I always think March should be warmer than this, you know?

PAM. Yeah. It seems like you wait all winter, and then it sounds like spring, but it's always so cold really.

SHEILA. I know.

JANET. And we wear these little jackets and pretend we're not cold because it's March. (ALL laugh ever so lightly.)

SHEILA (after a pause). Thank you for coming, but you don't have to be here. You really don't.

PAM. We went by your house, but you were gone.

JANET. We thought of all the places you might be, and we knew you'd come here.

SHEILA. I just needed a little time to myself. To think a little. We always liked this place.

JANET. I know.

SHEILA. It's always so quiet up here. The first time I came here I thought it was too much . . . so quiet, eerie, just so quiet. Danny grinned and said, "What do you expect in a place like this?" And then he laughed that silly little laugh. (ALL laugh lightly.) He's like that. Make you laugh at the strangest things. After a while, I never even thought about this being what it is. It was just a place. Nice, quiet, kind of pretty. Sort of our place, you know. Somewhere to come, to get away from things for a while.

PAM. Yeah.

SHEILA (crossing to the stump). So we came here a lot. When it was warm enough. And we'd sit on this little hillside and talk, or watch the clouds, and make up names for the things and faces we'd see take shape up there. Sometimes tremendous formations, always moving and blending into one another; becoming someone or something else. A quiet, ever-changing kind of thing. We'd just sit back and watch it happen. You know?

JANET (crossing to SHEILA and touching her shoulders, with a little smile). Yes. I've done that, too. Never in a place like this. But I've watched them, too.

SHEILA (as she sits on the stump). We quit thinking of it as that. Not a cemetery at all . . . just a place. Danny used to point over there, down the hill where the markers start, and he said it was just a little town where people stayed, that's all. The markers became buildings and in the evening you could almost visualize a little town down there. You had the town, that little stream there, and that hillside over there untouched, waiting to become part of the town. Everything so neat, so practical, so obvious. (She turns to JANET and PAM with a faint smile.) I've never told anyone that. It sounds so crazy, doesn't it?

JANET (smiling softly, kindly). No.

SHEILA. I know it does. It sounds so silly, just so crazy to talk like that. (She moves to the bench.) I can't tell you the hours we spent just sitting here, leaning against this old bench. Just talking, laughing, or sometimes not talking at all. Just listening and being quiet. (JANET and PAM nervously exchange glances.)

JANET. Sheila, it's cold. We should go now.

SHEILA. We used to look for lucky clovers here. Four-leaf clovers, you know? I guess everyone's done that.

JANET. Yeah.

SHEILA. I told Danny you couldn't find luck in a place like this, and he said you could find luck about anywhere.

JANET. Sheila?

SHEILA. Danny knew this saying about luck.

PAM (still looking out). Janet's right. It's cold, Sheila. Shouldn't you go now?

SHEILA (quietly reciting). "A clover's luck doubles by simply sharing/An act of kindness, an act of caring./For we are taught from up above/That the greatest act/is an act of love." (JANET crosses to SHEILA.) We only found one. (She struggles.) I have it. It's on this chain he gave me. (She sits on the corner of the bench, lowers her head, and begins to cry quietly.)

JANET. Don't, Sheila. (She sits by SHEILA and puts her arms around her.) Please don't.

PAM (kindly). Let's go. You need to go now, Sheila.

JANET. Please, Sheila. Leave with us.

SHEILA. I'm all right. You go on. I need a few more minutes.

PAM. You should go with us now.

SHEILA (moving away). No. Really. It's all right. You go ahead. I'll leave soon.

JANET. You shouldn't be here, Sheila.

SHEILA. It's all right.

JANET. No, it isn't. You ought to leave.

SHEILA. I won't be here long, I promise.

JANET. That's not what I'm talking about, Sheila.

SHEILA. What do you mean?

JANET. I mean Patsy, Steve and Tony. They're looking for you.

SHEILA. What?

JANET. They called my house. When you weren't home, they called me.

SHEILA. They did?

JANET. Yes. And I know they'll come here.

PAM. They all know this is where you and Danny would come.

JANET. They'll be here, Sheila.

SHEILA. No, they wouldn't.

JANET. They will. They think you've been talking.

PAM. They think you talked to the police.

SHEILA. I haven't talked to anyone. I haven't seen anyone.

PAM. Patsy said you were at the chapel last night.

SHEILA. Patsy?

JANET. Yes. When Tony called, he said Patsy had seen you, and that you were talking to David.

PAM. Patsy was across the street watching. She said she saw you.

SHEILA. I didn't go in. I couldn't. (A pause.) I just couldn't go inside.

PAM. But you did go?

SHEILA. Yes.

JANET. And you talked to David?

SHEILA. He's Danny's brother, Janet. And I did talk to him. He was on the porch when he saw me standing out front. He came to the street and we talked. For only a minute, and then I left. I couldn't go in.

JANET. Well, all that bunch thinks you talked about what happened.

SHEILA. They're wrong.

JANET. Well, they're trying to find you.

SHEILA (moving away). I'll leave in a minute. They won't find me here.

JANET. I don't trust them, Sheila. You know how they are. I don't trust them.

SHEILA. You all go on now. They won't bother me.

PAM. I think you're wrong.

SHEILA. You all go on. Don't worry.

(DAVID enters upstage and quietly moves into the scene.)

JANET. At least let us wait for you.

SHEILA. What?

JANET. We'll wait in the car. Okay?

SHEILA. You don't have to do that.

JANET. We want to.

PAM. We'll wait at the entrance. Okay?

SHEILA. All right. If you want. Just give me a few more minutes. I just want . . . (She sees DAVID.) Hello, David.

DAVID. Hello.

PAM and JANET. Hello.

DAVID. Hi. (An awkward pause.)

SHEILA. We were about to leave.

DAVID. I see.

JANET (after another pause). David, we're all sorry about Danny. (PAM nods agreement. Another awkward moment.)

DAVID (breaking the silence). Yes.

SHEILA. We're leaving now, David.

PAM. Yes, we were just going.

DAVID. Could I talk to you, Sheila?

SHEILA. What?

DAVID. For just a moment?

JANET. We were just leaving, David.

SHEILA. Yes, we were about to . . .

DAVID. Just a minute or two? Sheila, I really would like to talk for a moment . . . if you could just stay a minute.

SHEILA. Well, I don't . . .

DAVID. Please. Just a minute?

SHEILA (after a pause and an exchange of glances with JANET and PAM). Okay, David. I'll stay.

JANET. Sheila?

SHEILA. I'll just be a minute, Janet.

PAM. Sheila, I think you . . .

SHEILA (crossing to PAM and JANET). I'll just be a minute. Wait for me. I'll just be a minute.

JANET (after a pause). Okay. We'll be waiting. (As she starts out). Goodbye, David.

PAM. Goodbye.

DAVID. Goodbye. (JANET and PAM exit. SHEILA quietly sits on the bench as DAVID moves C, away from her. There is silence which is finally broken by DAVID.) Thank you for staying.

SHEILA. Sure. (DAVID stares ahead quietly.) You knew about this place?

DAVID. Oh, yes. I used to come here a lot.

SHEILA. You did?

DAVID (after a pause). When Dad first died. I'd just come up here and sit for awhile. Sit and listen. So quiet.

SHEILA. You did that?

DAVID. Yes. Sometimes. I could somehow never go down there . . . with the markers and all. I made it this far, and it was so quiet, so isolated, and this is as far as I ever wanted to go.

SHEILA. I see.

DAVID. And then one day, Danny followed me up here. I didn't hear him. I just sensed a presence. When I turned, there was Danny with a scared kind of look on his face, staring over the hill there. "It's so quiet," he said. I just took him by the shoulders and said, "What'd you expect in a place like this?" We both laughed a little and then we sat till the sun was nearly down. For some time after we would come up here whenever we needed a little time alone. We just called it the quiet place. Our special quiet place.

SHEILA. Then you first brought him here?

DAVID. In a way, I guess. He followed me that day.

SHEILA. And it became your place.

DAVID. Yes. I didn't want him to be afraid, you see. I didn't want him to be afraid to come here. He had a hard time when Dad died. I just didn't want him to be afraid.

SHEILA. And you?

DAVID. Me?

SHEILA. You said this was as far as you would ever go.

DAVID. It was as far as I needed to go. I wasn't afraid. I just didn't need to go down there. Everything I needed to feel, I could feel from here. Do you understand?

SHEILA. I think so.

DAVID. There was no reason to go. I could feel it from here. (A pause. DAVID stares over the hill, while SHEILA looks at him kindly.)

SHEILA. He talked of you often.

DAVID. He did?

SHEILA. Yes. Especially when you first went away to school. He missed you a lot.

DAVID. I missed him.

SHEILA. He loved it when you came home.

DAVID. So did I. (A pause.) I'm afraid I couldn't get here as often as I wanted to. Several hundred miles, you know.

SHEILA. Yes.

DAVID. It just seemed to get more difficult to find the time to get here. So I couldn't come as often as I used to, like last year.

SHEILA. Well, Danny understood that. He knew that.

DAVID. I somehow couldn't seem to find the time. (A pause.) I guess it's always like that, isn't it? People looking back saying, "I should have found the time."

SHEILA (quietly). Yes.

DAVID (after a slight pause). You didn't come in last night.

SHEILA. No.

DAVID. There were a lot of people there then.

SHEILA. I know.

DAVID. I think Mom would like to have seen you.

SHEILA. I'll see her later. I just couldn't go in.

DAVID (quietly). I know.

SHEILA. Those flowers. I can't stand the smell. I always feel so smothered. And I knew I really shouldn't go in.

DAVID (after a pause). Sheila, I don't understand what's happened. (Another pause.) I'm having real trouble understanding what's happened here.

SHEILA. Yes.

DAVID. Can you help me?

SHEILA. What?

DAVID (moving close to SHEILA). Can you help me?

SHEILA. I don't know.

DAVID. Will you help me, Sheila? Tell me what you know. Will you?

SHEILA (quietly). All right.

DAVID. Thank you.

SHEILA. I really don't know what to say, David. Danny and I didn't see much of each other lately.

DAVID. But you were at the party?

SHEILA. Well, yes. But that was the first time in a long time . . . almost eight weeks.

DAVID. Eight weeks?

SHEILA. Yes. The party was the first time I had seen him in a long time.

DAVID (after a pause). Well, what happened?

SHEILA. There was this crowd at school that Danny sort of fell in with, and we began to see less of each other.

DAVID. What about this crowd?

SHEILA. Just some kids. They used to tease Danny some, like they did a lot of people. Me. They did it to me, too. Just this bunch of loud kids that rode him a lot, about being cool and all that. You know.

DAVID. And?

SHEILA. And so, for some reason, this really started to bother

Danny and he somehow got mixed up with them, trying to prove he could do things and all.

DAVID. Things?

SHEILA. You know.

DAVID. No. Tell me.

SHEILA. You know, David.

DAVID. Tell me. Drugs? Is that what you're saying?

SHEILA. David.

DAVID. Is it? Is that what you mean?

SHEILA (quietly). Yes.

DAVID (after a pause). Who the hell's this crowd?

SHEILA. Just some kids. They run together. Always hang out together at school and everywhere.

DAVID. And they're all into this?

SHEILA. Yes.

DAVID. At school? It's like this at school?

SHEILA. Well . . . yes.

DAVID. They do this stuff at school, too?

SHEILA. Sometimes. Whenever they want, I guess.

DAVID. Damn.

SHEILA. David, I know Danny didn't realize what he was getting into. I know that. I hope you'll believe that, David.

DAVID. I want to.

SHEILA. Believe me. He just didn't know. It all just happened so fast. He didn't realize.

DAVID. I guess not.

SHEILA. He was not like them, David. He wasn't. I don't know why, but he just got pulled in like so many others have. He just got pulled into it.

DAVID. But you didn't.

SHEILA (quietly). No. But almost. (She moves away.) David, the pressure is very heavy sometimes. Even when it's not a bunch like those who got to Danny, there are lots of other kids who are doing the same kind of thing and just doing a better job of keeping it a secret. That's just the way it is. And if you knew some of the kids I'm talking about, you just wouldn't believe it. I'm talking about people you wouldn't even believe. And it's like that a lot. And everybody expects you to try things, and it's very hard. So, Danny is just like a lot of other kids who somehow have given in to this thing. And it's just real hard, David.

DAVID. What about the party?

SHEILA. The party?

DAVID. You saw Danny that night?

SHEILA. Yes. I had decided that I wanted to see Danny, no matter what, so I went to the party. And I found Danny, and he was with those kids. He seemed glad to see me . . . really glad to see me, and he even grabbed me and swung me around a little bit. He was really glad to see me, and I was glad I had gone as soon as he acted like that. So, he asked me to drink something with him, so I got a beer and two or three times I pretended to get others so everyone would think I was really drinking.

DAVID. Danny was drinking, too?

SHEILA. Yes. He had been drinking.

DAVID. And the drugs, too?

SHEILA. He didn't mean for that to happen. I know he didn't. He said his head hurt and they told him to take some more pills.

DAVID. More pills?

SHEILA. Yes. He had some earlier, before I got there. They were teasing him about his pain, and kept telling him to take those others and there'd be no pain. And he did. (About to cry.) And later it happened. He fell asleep. And I stayed with him . . . there . . . and then he just couldn't . . . wake up . . . it happened . . . he couldn't wake up . . . (She stands, holding back tears.) It was just an accident . . . it just . . . happened. (There is silence.) That's all, David. I'm sure Danny never knew . . . about it. I know he didn't realize what was happening . . . he never really . . . knew. He was just having fun . . . and the next thing we know, this happened. And that's all I know to say, David. (A pause. DAVID stares over the hill. SHEILA struggles hard not to cry.)

DAVID. Thank you for talking to me, Sheila.

SHEILA (quietly). It's all right.

DAVID. I have to go now.

SHEILA. Me, too.

DAVID (still staring over the hill). I need to go down there now. To the lot. I need to . . . check things for the fune . . . for tomorrow. (After a pause.) Thank you, Sheila. (SHEILA fights back tears and nods. DAVID goes over the hill toward the markers. SHEILA stares after him for a moment, then sits on the end of the bench. She stares straight ahead in silence.)

(PATSY, TONY and STEVE enter and stop when they see SHEILA. ALL move to SHEILA.)

PATSY. Sheila.

SHEILA. I'm comin' . . . (She realizes it is not her friends and rises.) What are you doing here?

TONY. We want to talk.

SHEILA. You have no business here.

TONY. We want to talk to you.

SHEILA. You have no right coming here.

PATSY. We just want to talk.

TONY. There's a few things we need to know.

SHEILA. I have nothing to say to you. Any of you.

PATSY. You need to talk to us, Sheila.

SHEILA. I don't want to talk to you.

TONY (firmly). Well, you're gonna talk.

PATSY. Tony.

TONY. You are gonna talk to us, Sheila. You are.

STEVE. Tony, lighten up.

TONY. Butt out.

STEVE. Let Patsy talk, Tony. That's all. Let Patsy talk.

TONY (after a pause, to PATSY). Go ahead.

PATSY (after a pause, she nears SHEILA). We know you're upset about Danny. (SHEILA stares coldly at PATSY.) We all are. Nobody wanted this to happen.

STEVE. That's right, Sheila. We're all sorry about this.

PATSY. It's just one of those things, you know.

SHEILA. One of those things? For God's sake, Patsy.

TONY. That's right. Just one of those things. Nobody expected this to happen.

STEVE (sincerely). It was an accident, Sheila.

SHEILA (starting to leave). I have to go.

TONY (stepping in). Not yet.

SHEILA. Get out of my way.

PATSY. We have to talk first.

SHEILA. I told you, I have nothing to say to you. I don't want to talk to you. (She moves away from the OTHERS.)

PATSY. Look, Sheila. We all know you had this thing for Danny. We all know that.

SHEILA. Thing? What do you mean, thing? God, just stop. Leave me alone and stop.

TONY. Patsy, get to the point.

SHEILA. Why don't you all just leave, or let me leave. Just get out of my way.

PATSY. Sheila, you were at the party, too.

TONY. That's right.

PATSY. So you're a part of what went on there.

TONY. You're a part of what happened.

SHEILA. I am not.

PATSY. Yes.

TONY. Oh, yes, Sheila, you are.

SHEILA. I was at that party, but I am not part of what you did.

TONY. Oh . . . wait a minute. That's what I thought you would say, "what we did." Just what do you mean when you make a statement like that?

STEVE. Tony, come on. Can't we just talk?

TONY. Hey . . . I am talking. You hear me? I am talking! (There is silence. STEVE moves to one side.) You trying to say you ain't part of what happened at the party? That right, Sheila?

SHEILA. That's right.

PATSY. You were there. You're a part of it.

TONY. You were with him.

PATSY. You were drinking with him.

SHEILA. I was not drinking with him.

TONY. Hey, now, we all know better.

PATSY. You drank beer with him all night.

SHEILA. I drank a half a beer the whole time I was there.

TONY. You're lying.

SHEILA. I only pretended to drink.

PATSY. That's not the way we saw it, is it?

TONY. No. (He turns to STEVE.) Is it, Steve?

STEVE. No.

SHEILA. Well, that's the way it was. The whole time I was pretending so Danny would think I was drinking.

PATSY. Pretending?

SHEILA. I wanted Danny to leave with me. I just wanted to

get him out of there.

PATSY. Why didn't you just ask him to leave?

TONY. That's right. Why didn't you just ask him to leave, Sheila?

SHEILA (quietly). I did.

TONY. Yeah?

SHEILA. He wouldn't go.

TONY. That's right. He wouldn't go. He was having too much fun.

PATSY. He didn't want to leave, did he?

SHEILA. He couldn't leave. He was in no shape to leave.

TONY. The truth is he was having a damned good time and he didn't want to leave all the fun. Ain't that right?

SHEILA. No.

PATSY. Tony's right, Sheila. He's telling the truth.

SHEILA. Truth.

PATSY. That's right.

TONY. He was having fun, and you were about to spoil it. That's all. That's all.

STEVE. Tony.

TONY. Shut up! (SHEILA moves away from the OTHERS.)

PATSY. Who have you been talking to, Sheila?

SHEILA. What?

TONY (moving in). Who all you been talking to? About what happened?

SHEILA. No one.

PATSY. I saw you last night. (SHEILA doesn't answer.) With David. (SHEILA still doesn't answer.)

TONY. We know you went down there. To that chapel. Who all did you talk to?

SHEILA. No one. I didn't even go in.

PATSY. You talked to David?

SHEILA. For only a minute.
PATSY. What did you talk about?
SHEILA. Nothing.
TONY. Nothing? You talked about nothing?
SHEILA. That's right.
PATSY. You talk about us?
SHEILA. No.
TONY. You sure?
SHEILA (moving away). For God's sake, yes. I'm sure.
PATSY. What did you talk about?
SHEILA. This is ridiculous. I'm leaving.
TONY (moving in front of SHEILA). Not yet.
SHEILA. Get out of my way.
STEVE. Tony.
TONY. Shut up!
SHEILA (trying to hide her fear). I want to leave.
PATSY. First we need to get something clear. We want to make sure that we're all saying the same thing.
SHEILA. Same thing?
PATSY. Look, Sheila, let's just get to it. What happened to Danny is bad. We're all sorry. We wish it hadn't happened, but it did. People are asking questions. They're gonna ask more. After tomorrow, the police will be asking around, and we all know that. So, we all need our stories to be straight.
SHEILA. And just what are you saying, Patsy?
PATSY. I'm saying that we should all let this thing end. All of us answer the questions with the same story and let this damned thing end.
TONY. She's right. Let's let it end.
PATSY. So when you do talk to people . . . we just need to make sure we all see it the same way.
SHEILA. And just how is that?

PATSY. The way it happened.

TONY. He drank too much, and then he got to messin' with those pills.

SHEILA. Pills?

TONY. Yeah. We didn't know he was messing with those pills.

PATSY. We just thought he was drinking a little beer, like everyone else.

SHEILA. That's a lie.

TONY. But Danny was like that. You never knew what he would do. Ain't that right, Patsy?

PATSY. Yeah.

TONY. So the next thing we know, he's takin' these pills. And that's not good. We all know that. Right, Steve?

STEVE (quietly). Right.

TONY. What's that?

STEVE. Right.

PATSY. I mean, no one expected him to do a thing like that. Not with the beer and all.

SHEILA. I see.

PATSY. Good. Then we all agree about it.

SHEILA. I mean I see what you're doing.

TONY. We're telling the truth, Sheila. And all of this will come to an end and things will get back to normal for all of us. We're all just sorry it ever happened.

PATSY. You see?

SHEILA (speaking quietly and deliberately through her fear). I'll tell you what I see. I see liars and hypocrites. Every damned one of you.

TONY. Hey, now. I think you should watch that.

SHEILA. And I think you should really face the truth. You talked about truth. Well, I'll tell you what truth is. The truth is, Danny is dead because of you.

TONY. Sheila.

SHEILA. It's true! You gave Danny those pills. I saw that with my own eyes.

TONY. Is that what you saw, Patsy? Did I give him the pills? Did I?

PATSY. No.

SHEILA. You did it, too. Patsy, I saw you both. For God's sake, I was there. Remember?

TONY. Is that what you remember, Patsy? Steve? (STEVE stands silently with his head down.)

PATSY. No. That's not what I remember at all.

SHEILA. Well, you're both lying. We all know that.

TONY. We didn't give nobody any pills.

SHEILA (fearful, but with piercing honesty). Everybody knows about you, Tony. That's all you do . . . mess with that stuff. Everybody knows about you.

PATSY. He didn't give no one any pills.

SHEILA. You're just as bad, Patsy. You and Tony . . . you're just alike! You're always into something, and this time look what's happened!

STEVE. Maybe we should go.

TONY. Not yet.

STEVE. We could talk later. This is no good.

SHEILA. What did you expect?

TONY. We expect you to talk like you got a little sense, instead of like this.

PATSY. All we want is to know that you are seeing our point.

SHEILA. Oh, I see it.

TONY. We just want to know that you're not going to get us involved.

SHEILA. Get you involved?

TONY. That's right.

SHEILA. What is wrong with you, Tony? Get you involved?

PATSY. You know what we mean, Sheila.

SHEILA. Yeah, I know what you mean. You want me to pretend that this didn't happen. That Danny's death was all his own fault. You want me to lie and pretend that I didn't see what I saw. You expect me not to admit what I know really happened.

TONY. Look, Sheila. I'm telling you right now that you are way out of line to try to drag us into this. Danny drank the booze. Danny took the pills. No one forced him to do it. He just did it.

SHEILA. That's a lie. You gave him the pills. You helped Danny take his own life by your goading and taunting. You know it and you have to face it.

PATSY. Your word against ours, Sheila. And there are three of us who say you are lying.

TONY. Yeah. (He pauses and walks away from SHEILA.) Maybe you're the one with the pills. Maybe you were the one. Right, Patsy? Right, Steve?

PATSY. Right.

TONY. Steve? Right?

STEVE. I don't know.

TONY. Well, you'd better know, and you'd better know real fast.

STEVE. I think we should go. Let's talk another time.

TONY. Are you with us or not?

STEVE. Yeah, but . . .

PATSY. Look, Sheila. Can't we just agree to let it all drop? Just let it all end.

TONY. That's all we're asking.

SHEILA. No, that's not what you're asking. You're asking me to say you have no responsibility here. You're asking me to absolve you from what happened to Danny. Well, I can't do that.

Even if I never told anyone what I know happened, that wouldn't change your part in this. That's something that will never change, no matter what anyone says or does. You're going to have to live with that all your lives. Danny is dead. You gave him the pills. Those are the facts and you're going to have to face that. Don't expect me to lie for you. And don't try to threaten me with that line about my having the pills.

STEVE. We don't mean to threaten, Sheila.

SHEILA. Maybe not you, Steve. But I know what Tony and Patsy are saying. I know very well.

TONY. Then you ought to keep your mouth shut.

SHEILA (her anger growing). Let me tell you something . Let me make this clear to all of you. I will not be frightened into telling lies for you. I will tell the truth. I owe that to Danny. I owe him the truth.

PATSY. Sheila.

SHEILA. I don't understand you. I don't understand any of you, and I will not defend you or what you stand for.

TONY. You're making a big mistake, Sheila.

SHEILA. My mistake was not trying harder to get Danny away from all of you. I should never have stopped trying. That was my mistake.

STEVE. Let's go.

TONY. A mistake, Sheila.

SHEILA. I'll not make it worse by letting you off scott-free. You'll never see a day in jail, you'll never go to court. But I'll not make it easier for you by hiding the truth. Every time you see me, I want you to think of Danny. I want you to remember what happened because of you.

PATSY. You can't blame us!

SHEILA. No one has to blame you. It's just there. The blame

is there, now live with it.

TONY. Listen to me, Sheila!

SHEILA (almost crying). No, you listen to me, mister tough guy. Always the tough guy. The big, bad guy. Well, don't you ever let up? Is that really you . . . the real Tony? When do you quit this crap? What does it take for you to be a real person in a real world? What does it take to stop all this crap you people do?

PATSY. Listen.

SHEILA. Patsy, look at you! Look at what has happened to you. Look at what you've become! Danny is dead. Tomorrow they will bring him here and he will lie here from now on. I will never see him again. He'll not ever be around again. Never! He is gone forever. And what are you all doing? Facing this like real people? No, you act like something from some movie . . . playing out these damned roles, never facing what's really happened. This gang crap. These images! It's really sad, Patsy. It's sad!

TONY. I think you have said enough.

SHEILA. I have said the truth.

TONY (his anger growing). Well, I'm telling you that you had better not drag me into this.

SHEILA. You don't scare me.

TONY (angrier still). You just watch what you say. You hear?

SHEILA. I'm not afraid of you.

TONY (taking SHEILA by the arm). Maybe you ought to be.

STEVE. Tony!

SHEILA. You can't frighten me. You can beat me, but you can't make me lie.

PATSY. Tony, don't do anything.

TONY. I'm telling you to watch what you say!

SHEILA (almost in tears). Go ahead. Hit me, Tony. That's

your style, isn't it? That's your image.

TONY. Shut up!

SHEILA. Keep playing that game, Tony!

TONY (jerking Sheila's arm). I told you to shut up!

STEVE (moving to the OTHERS). Tony, stop. Leave her alone.

SHEILA (crying now). You can't hurt me! Nothing you can do will hurt me!

TONY. I'm telling you for the last time.

SHEILA. You're telling me nothing!

PATSY. Tony, don't.

SHEILA. Nothing!

STEVE. Tony!

TONY. Go on! Keep sticking up for him! He deserved a bitch like you! (SHEILA breaks Tony's hold and slaps TONY hard across the face. TONY is stunned. Before TONY can react, STEVE and PATSY grab him. SHEILA breaks away and sits on the bench, crying. TONY breaks to the other side and stops. There is a terrible silence broken only by an occasional sound from SHEILA as she struggles to control her crying.)

PATSY (after a long pause). Let's go. Come on, Tony. Let's go.

STEVE. Tony, let's leave.

PATSY. Please, Tony.

TONY (after a pause). Yeah. (ALL except SHEILA leave. Nearly out, TONY stops and turns toward SHEILA. He takes a step toward her and raises his arm in a gesture as if to speak. Instead, the silence continues. PATSY goes to TONY, takes him by the elbow, and BOTH exit. STEVE follows. SHEILA slowly stops crying.)

(DAVID enters from the cemetery. He sees SHEILA and comes down to her.)

DAVID. Still here?

SHEILA (turning to DAVID). Yes.

DAVID. You've been here a long time.

SHEILA. Not really.

DAVID. Would you like a ride?

SHEILA (rising and moving away). No, thank you. I'll be here a few more minutes.

DAVID. You sure? I'd be glad to take you home.

SHEILA. No, thanks. I have friends waiting. I'll be leaving in a minute.

DAVID (kindly). All right. Well, I have to be going.

SHEILA (quietly). Goodbye.

DAVID. Goodbye. (He turns to leave, then stops and turns back to SHEILA.) Will you be here tomorrow?

SHEILA. What?

DAVID. Will you be attending tomorrow?

SHEILA. I don't know.

DAVID. You might want to come.

SHEILA (after a pause, quietly and with difficulty). I won't need to be here . . . to feel what I need to feel . . . you know what I mean?

DAVID (crossing to SHEILA and gently touching her shoulder). Yes. Yes, I do. (He turns to leave). Goodbye, Sheila.

SHEILA. Goodbye. (DAVID leaves. She wipes her eyes and stares over the hill toward the lot. After a moment, she crosses back to the bench, removes the chain necklace, thoughtfully places it on the ground by the bench, rises, and speaks quietly.) Goodbye. (She exits slowly against the sound of the wind and the birds.)

CURTAIN

DIRECTOR'S NOTES

DIRECTOR'S NOTES

DIRECTOR'S NOTES

DIRECTOR'S NOTES

DIRECTOR'S NOTES